and Beyond

ay for Babies and Children

ark making

Baby and Beyond - Mark making

ISBN 1 905019 78 5

© Featherstone Education Ltd, 2006

Text © Sally Featherstone and Liz Williams, 2006; Illustrations © Martha Hardy, 2006; Series Editor, Sally Featherstone

First published in the UK, October 2006

'Baby and Beyond' is a trade mark of Featherstone Education Ltd

Published in the United Kingdom by

Featherstone Education Ltd, 44 - 46 High Street, Husbands Bosworth, Leicestershire, LE17 6LP

Printed in the UK on paper produced in the European Union from managed, sustainable forests

Contents

Baby and Beyond

A series of books for practitioners working with children from Birth to Three and beyond

This book gives ideas for introducing and extending mark making activities and experiences for babies and young children. Each page spread contains a range of experiences and a selection of ideas for each of the four developmental stages of the Birth to Three Matters Framework, and extends this progression into the early Stepping Stones for the Foundation Stage:

Young Babies -
Heads Up, Lookers
and Communicators
0-8 months

Babies -
Sitters, Standers and
Explorers
8-18 months

Young Children -
Movers, Shakers and
Players
18-24 months

Children -
Walkers, Talkers and
Pretenders
24-36 months

Foundation Stage -
Yellow Stepping
Stone and beyond
Foundation 1 and 2

Young babies need to have access to the experiences at floor level, on an adult's knee and in their arms, so plan for all these. Babies and children also need the company and stimulation of adults if they are to extend their play into thinking and learning. As they move through the developmental stages, the experiences can be offered in differing ways and at differing heights - lying down, sitting (both propped and independent), kneeling, standing - and different children will develop preferences for some of these. Some older children will still enjoy working lying down, while some very young children will be determined to sit or stand even before they are able to do it alone! Using small and large trays (e.g. plant and builders' trays) is a simple but effective way of enabling easy access to these kinds of play for all babies and children.

Adult/child interaction is essential at all levels to encourage children's learning and development. Talking with and listening to babies and children are also vital in supporting and developing self-esteem. Observing their play is essential for recognising both their achievements and their needs, so you can plan for future learning.

The experiences with mark making materials described in this book encourage development and learning through active play using all the senses. Enhancing experiences of mark making from babyhood will encourage children's independence and involvement in communication through meaningful marks.

All babies and children benefit from outdoor learning experiences, so we have not restricted the materials and activities to use indoors. Many early experiences of mark making are enhanced by offering them out of doors, and some children actually learn better in a garden. Some activities are messy, some need space, and we suggest that the youngest babies and children will benefit from watching older children at work with mark making materials. This gives plenty of real life modelling, which babies and children find fascinating, and should be a feature of high quality learning.

At the heart of meaningful mark making is communication, and the start of communication is in the use of expressive sounds, simple talk, naming, expression and response to babies first sounds. Spend time with babies, listening to them, describing what you are doing together, and responding to their first efforts at communication. Observation is the key to knowing when to move to the next stage in learning.

Older babies and children will benefit from access to a wide range of mark making experiences and equipment in all situations and on all sorts of surfaces. A mark making and writing area should be available on free access as soon as children are able to move around and choose what they do. This area needs adult support and presence, so you can watch, help, suggest and model being a writer. Try not to dominate or interfere in children's free play and independent activities!

Young babies (0-8 months)	Babies (8-18 months)	Young children (18-24 months)	Children (24-36 months)	Foundation 1&2 (over 3)

Heads Up, Lookers and Communicators	Sitters, Standers and Explorers	Movers, Shakers and Players	Walkers, Talkers and Pretenders	Moving on into the Foundation Stage

Food

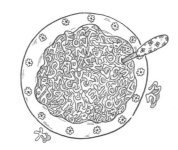

Food is usually the first mark-making substance encountered by babies and 'playing with food', although it may not be encouraged by adults, is an abiding activity throughout childhood. With fingers first, then using utensils or even a piece of bread, making marks and patterns in food helps finger and hand control.

Sauce, pudding or yogurt spilt on the tray of a chair can be pushed, trailed or poked by an index finger or a fist. Patting or smearing are also movements that young babies will use to move food around on a tray or table surface. It is sometimes tempting to stop children playing with food with their fingers, but it is an essential stage in hand and finger control, so the more independent they get, the better it is - messy is good for this purpose!

Heads Up, Lookers and Communicators

Older babies and children will still be fascinated by spilt food or food presented as malleable materials for learning. Whipped cream, jelly, custard, rice pudding and mashed potato all give opportunities for squeezing, squashing and pounding. Picking up small food items is a good way to encourage the pincer grip needed later for holding mark making instruments. Try raisins, small pasta shapes, vegetable sticks, peas, beans etc.

Sitters, Standers and Explorers

Young children (18-24 months)

Offer dough for making simple jam tarts, cheese straws, scones, buns and bread. Pounding, squeezing and rolling all help hand control and prepare children for using mark making tools. Cooked spaghetti sticks to paper and can be arranged in patterns and shapes (try adding some food colouring to the cooking water to make coloured spaghetti or shapes). Serving themselves or others by spooning food and pouring drinks will help with control.

Movers, Shakers and Players

Children (24-36 months)

At snack time offer children carrots, celery, peppers and other vegetables cut into sticks, with yogurt, hummus, cream cheese or tomato salsa. This will help with hand control and finger grip. Continue to offer malleable and finger foods at meal times - pasta, breadsticks, small fruit such as grapes and raisins, peas - or food cut into small pieces (cheese, bread, fresh fruit, tiny sandwiches etc). Rolling and cutting dough into shapes also helps control.

Walkers, Talkers and Pretenders

Foundation 1&2 (over 3)

Decorating ready made biscuits is a quick and easy way to make a special snack - try icing sweet biscuits with icing pens, or savoury crackers with cream cheese. Then use tweezers to decorate with hundreds and thousands or edible seeds. Use pipettes to add food colouring to drinking water a drop at a time. Make words and names with alphabetti spaghetti. Make marks and letters in flour in a shallow tray. Drizzle honey on yogurt or jam on rice pudding.

Moving on into the Foundation Stage

Finger paint

Finger paint comes in a range of different colours and consistencies. Make sure it is safe for very young children to use (it may get eaten!). Some children may need encouragement to get their hands painty, so go gently and praise their efforts. Start early so babies get used to paint from an early stage.

Young babies (0-8 months)

Put a small amount of finger paint on a tray where a baby can reach it from your knee or as they lie on the floor. Stay with them as they experiment, to make sure they don't eat too much! Show them how to make marks by using your fingers to move the paint over the tray or table. Short sessions are much more effective with babies, so don't go on too long, and if the individual baby becomes anxious, stop.

Heads Up, Lookers and Communicators

Babies (8-18 months)

Standing babies may like to use finger paint on a vertical surface such as an unbreakable mirror or a sheet of thick plastic or perspex. It may be wise to remove clothing and just let them work in a nappy for this activity, and limit the number of colours. You can also put paint in trays on a table or the floor, for babies to reach, pat, poke, and make marks. Adding a bit of moisturiser to the paint makes it easier to remove from skin and clothes.

Sitters, Standers and Explorers

Young children (18-24 months)

At this stage, young children may like to use finger paint to decorate dolls, small world animals, plastic bricks, toy cars etc.

Don't use brushes, encourage them to isolate their index fingers so they can begin to make patterns, dots and spots. Use finger paint outside too, on paths and walls, or on a shower curtain suspended from a wall or fence. Take some photos of the children at work before washing the paint away with a hose.

Movers, Shakers and Players

Children (24-36 months)

At this stage, children will love to work standing at a table with a friend to talk to. Add finger paint to gloop and foam to make different colours and textures (start with the foam, then just add a small blob of paint so the children can mix it in themselves). If you work on a dark surface, the children will soon discover that they can make patterns and marks appear as their fingers push through the painty foam, exposing the table top.

Walkers, Talkers and Pretenders

Foundation 1&2 (over 3)

Continue to offer finger paint as a table top experience, and occasionally show the children how they can take a print by carefully laying paper over their patterns and rubbing gently before peeling back the paper to reveal the print. Talk about why the picture, pattern or letter-like marks come out back to front on the print. Encourage children to develop mark making by painting shapes, patterns, lines etc. Model left to right movement in patterns.

Moving on into the Foundation Stage

11

Water

Water is a great experience for mark making - it dries easily, can be used anywhere and children love it! Use these features by offering water painting as a child initiated activity whenever you can, specially outside. Get cheap packs of decorating paintbrushes from DIY stores and offer lots of different sizes.

Young babies (0-8 months)

Sit with babies and drizzle your hands in warm water, watching the drips drop from your fingers onto the surface of the water. Try offering a shallow bowl of warm water for babies to dip their hands in and drip on black paper or an unbreakable mirror laid flat on the floor. Let babies pat wet hands and fingers on table tops and worktops. Sit them in a builder's tray with a very shallow amount of water so they can splash and pat the water on a warm day outside!).

Heads Up, Lookers and Communicators

Babies (8-18 months)

When babies begin to stand and lean, try a low table covered with a plastic shower curtain or black paper for dripping and patting water on a flat surface. Hold babies so they can poke and follow drops of water on window panes inside or out. Warm, bubbly water and sponges encourage squeezing, splashing and smearing. Simple containers for filling and emptying will help them to improve hand control.

Sitters, Standers and Explorers

Young children (18-24 months)

Once children are steady on their feet, offer small plastic buckets of water and brushes or sponges for outdoor painting on walls, doors and paving stones. Add plenty of pouring and scooping equipment to water trays - plastic bottles, funnels and tubes will all help young children to develop hand, wrist and finger movements ready for mark making. Try dripping water from fingers and hands onto shallow trays of dry sand, flour or powder paint.

Movers, Shakers and Players

Children (24-36 months)

Offer plastic droppers and coloured water for dripping and dropping onto absorbent paper such as paper towels to make splodgy pictures. Clean the detailed parts of wheeled toys with small paintbrushes and soapy water. Watch raindrops falling on dry paths and pavements and scrape raindrops from windows with squeegees and scrapers. Washing equipment and dolls' clothes will strengthen hands and wrists for writing.

Walkers, Talkers and Pretenders

Foundation 1&2 (over 3)

As children's hand control improves, add very small bottles, funnels, tubes and spoons to water play, for filling and emptying with care. Provide access to water outside, so children can fill and empty their own watering cans and buckets. Water bottles with drinking tops make good water containers for making patterns and tracks on paths outside or absorbent paper indoors. Offer plastic pump bottles from liquid soap for adding water carefully to paint when mixing.

Moving on into the Foundation Stage

13

Chalk

Chalk is cheap, easily handled, makes marks with little effort, and is easily removed from surfaces with water. Look for large playground or pavement chalks in bargain shops as well as in educational supply catalogues. For suppliers of big square blocks of white chalk try Google 'playground chalk'. Add some small chalks too.

Young babies (0-8 months)

Babies will just need to feel the big blocks and sticks of chalk - their hands will not be strong enough to make marks. Take them to see older chidlren using the chalk indoors and outside, so they see how it works. Hold babies so they can see you making marks on a wall or the ground with big and small chalks.

Heads Up, Lookers and Communicators

Babies (8-18 months)

Cut paper into big circles and tape to the floor. Sit a baby in the middle with a small basket of chalks. Encourage them to chalk all round themselves; (if you cut a baby-sized hole in the middle of the paper, it will be easier for them to shuffle round as they work). You can also do this outside, direct onto paths and pavings. Indoors, you could tape black paper to a table and offer pale chalk colours so standing babies can share a mark making activity.

Sitters, Standers and Explorers

Young children (18-24 months)

Offer chalk for pattern and line making outside on walls and paths. Add a blackboard to your painting area for chalk work on a vertical surface. Use chalk to make paths and lines for children to walk and ride along on foot or on wheeled toys. Screw a long blackboard low down on an inside or outside wall for picture making. Using sponges and water to remove chalk from surfaces is almost as much fun as the chalking!

Movers, Shakers and Players

Children (24-36 months)

Use blackboard paint to make chalk boards on walls. You could also make a chalking space on the ground to encourage children to keep their chalk work in one place! Help the children to make roadways and lines to follow with small world cars and trucks. Make chalk footprints, or circles for jumping and throwing games. Start patterns for children to finish, and try to encourage them to work together on big murals on inside or outside walls.

Walkers, Talkers and Pretenders

Foundation 1&2 (over 3)

Older children can use chalk to make simple playground games such as number snakes, lines, hopscotch, arrows and circles, practising numbers and letters as they work. Offer chalk for making small world maps for farms, zoos, towns, airports, jungles etc. on the ground or on carpet remnants (these marks wipe off with a damp cloth). Show them how to do rubbings and follow or colour patterns on block paving or walls with small or playground chalk.

Moving on into the Foundation Stage

Pens and other markers

Pens and markers come in a wide range of types, colours and sizes. Try to offer a good selection to children at all stages of development, so they can choose which they will use. Check that the inks are washable - permanent pens will be difficult to remove from skin or clothing.

Young babies (0-8 months)

Give babies big pens (with tops on!) to hold, so they can get used to the feel of pens even before they can hold them to make a mark. Show them how pens make marks by making simple marks or shapes as they watch. Talk as you work, so you keep their attention and increase their concentration. Or take them to see older children using pens and markers indoors and outside to see how they are used.

Heads Up, Lookers and Communicators

Babies (8-18 months)

Once they can stand, babies love to do things in parallel, so completely cover a table with paper and offer all sorts of pens for a collaborative marking session over a day or two, where everyone can have a go. Sometimes offer big felt pens instead of paint for work at low easels, or instead of crayons in a mark making session. Use pens on all sorts of papers and cards, including boxes, cartons and sheets of plastic or foam.

Sitters, Standers and Explorers

Young children (18-24 months)

Cut drawing and painting paper into different shapes and sizes, and offer different types of paper for use with felt pens and markers (try tracing paper, wallpaper, textured and coloured paper in circles, strips, triangles and with wavy or fringed edges). Draw with felt pens, then drip water on for a first science investigation, or dip felt pens in water before drawing or making marks with them. Use dry wipe pens on white boards of all sizes.

Movers, Shakers and Players

Children (24-36 months)

At this stage, it's a good idea to offer fine felt pens as well as thicker ones. Some children love fine pens, and all children should have the chance to experiment with them. Big collaborative pictures are still fun to do at this stage, so put big sheets of paper on tables, on the floor or pin them to battens fixed to walls outside. Try tying several pens together with a strong elastic band for rainbow colours on paper, card or white boards.

Walkers, Talkers and Pretenders

Foundation 1&2 (over 3)

Make 'stained glass' pictures by using felt pens on tracing or greaseproof paper. When the drawing is complete, wipe over the back of the paper with a little cooking oil to make the colours even more glowing. Try fabric paints on small fabric squares and use to make a patchwork quilt picture. Make wet pictures by drawing on damp paper. Explore different sorts of pens, such as ones that change colour or erase each other. Use felt pens for mind mapping, brainstorming or making labelled diagrams or maps.

Moving on into the Foundation Stage

17

Gloop and foam

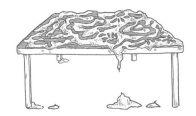

Make gloop with cornflour and water, mixed to a thin creamy consistency, or substitute with paint, spray cream or non-allergenic shaving foam. Clean these substances from surfaces using an old credit or loyalty card.

Stay with babies at all times when they are using these materials.

Put some gloop or foam in a small tray and let babies sit on your knee while they pat or poke it. Some babies don't like the feel of some things, so don't force them, just do it yourself and let them know you like it. You could also put these materials on the tray of a high chair or baby chair, but still stay close so it doesn't go in eyes or mouths.

Heads Up, Lookers and Communicators

Sit babies in builders' trays with gloop or foam. Sit with them while they play and encourage them to use hands, fingers (and feet) to make patterns in the gloop or foam. Put foam on a low table for standers and let them just use their hands to move the foam around. Watch what they do and look together at the marks they have made (a dark coloured surface will give better contrast). Model the use of a single finger, but don't insist on this!

Sitters, Standers and Explorers

Young children (18-24 months)

As young children get used to what foam and gloop can do, they will become more adventurous in the marks they make - when you sit with them, praise and encourage purposeful mark and pattern making. Put a small amount of ready mixed paint at the edge of foam play so children can colour their foam if they want to. Try running cars or animals through the foam, making tracks and prints.

Movers, Shakers and Players

Children (24-36 months)

Colour gloop and foam with paint or food colouring.

At this stage, children may be able to hold and manipulate simple tools in foam and gloop. Try making card combs, or using straws, small brushes or dried up felt pens. Use these to make patterns, shapes and zigzags. Show the children new shapes and patterns if they run out of ideas. Writing letters, specially those in their own names may emerge naturally - don't force it.

Walkers, Talkers and Pretenders

Foundation 1&2 (over 3)

Foams are ideal materials for practising all sorts of mark making. Stencils, plastic letters and numbers, stamps, sponges can all be used successfully to mark in the foam/gloop. Children can make their own 'combs' by cutting patterns and shapes out of the edges of pieces of card, and using these to make patterns. They can also practise writing letters, numbers, words and shapes in this forgiving material where errors can easily be erased. Individual containers of gloop or foam in a shallow rectangular plant saucer provide a good surface for such practice.

Moving on into the Foundation Stage

Printing and stampers

Printing and stamping provide endless fun for children and are good resources for strengthening hands and wrists, mark making and left to right direction. There are hundreds of different sorts of stampers (character, number, shape, letter, animal, nature, seasonal, holiday, borders etc) and they come in sponge, rubber, flat and roller.

Young babies (0-8 months)

Holding and looking at stampers will be a good start for babies. You could hold their hand gently in yours as you stamp together, but they almost certainly won't be able to connect the action with the result! Stamped sequences of large prints of simple outlines, patterns or shapes may attract their attention, specially if they offer a good contrast of black and white.

Heads Up, Lookers and Communicators

Babies (8-18 months)

Simple commercial stampers with large round handles to clutch may appeal to babies, but it's probably better to make your own stampers from big chunks of foam with flat trays of paint to dip them in. Cover a big low table with paper and let the babies stamp standing up. It's easier to manage if the paper is stuck down firmly.

Babies may also enjoy stamping with sponges and water on paths or walls out of doors.

Sitters, Standers and Explorers

Young children (18-24 months)

Continue making your own stampers from sponge or polystyrene, keeping them big enough to handle easily. You can also use household equipment such as potato mashers, net bags stuffed with foam, plastic sieves, cups and bowls to make prints with different sorts of paints. Get self-inking commercial stampers and make sure they are comfortable to hold and suitably large. Most children may find it easier to use stampers standing up.

Movers, Shakers and Players

Children (24-36 months)

Widen the range of sorts of stampers available to children at this stage. Add character, shape, and seasonal stamps, and encourage the children to use them for cards, letters and messages. Use them as borders for paintings and pictures, and stamp on large sheets of paper for wrapping paper or backing for displays. Free access stamping sessions will continue to strengthen hands, fingers and wrists.

Walkers, Talkers and Pretenders

Foundation 1&2 (over 3)

At this stage, children will enjoy adding letter, number and shape stamps to their repertoire. They can be offered as a resource for a mark making and writing table, for illustrating, bordering or decorating letters, labels, notes, messages. As children gain control of individual fingers, try 'finger stamps' on individual fingers, and experiment with repeating patterns, names, words and other labels. Date stamping their own paintings and other work is a huge time saver, enabling children to get on with the activity immediately.

Moving on into the Foundation Stage

21

Hands, feet and fingers

Hands, feet and fingers are the first mark makers - and they are free! If your setting is warm and safe, babies and young children can work barefoot for most of the day, and older children should continue to feel surfaces and materials with their hands, fingers AND feet. Make sure tactile experiences are included in your mark making plans

Young babies (0-8 months)

Playing finger songs and rhymes with babies will sensitise their hands and fingers and improve strength and grip. Add some toe tickling games as well, using a clean feather or something soft as you talk and sing to individual babies. Hold them so they can feel surfaces (such as sand, carpet, tiles, paint, gloop etc)and objects with their feet and hands. Hold things within their reach so they can touch and feel them as well as seeing them

Heads Up, Lookers and Communicators

Babies (8-18 months)

Give babies plenty of opportunities to feel natural surfaces with their feet - sand, gloop, paint, gravel, compost, mud, flour, cooked pasta etc. Offer lots of experiences for squidging and poking materials such as clay, dough, cooked pasta, jelly, so they can see AND feel the effects of their hands and feet on materials. Work with them as they pat and mould dough with palms, fingers and the heel of hands. Make painty hand prints with white paint on black paper.

Sitters, Standers and Explorers

Young children (18-24 months)

Finger paint is a great way to explore mark making with hands - try finger paint with feet on paper on the floor.

Make finger marks and trails in paint, gloop, wet and dry sand etc. Watch for footprints in mud, snow and water outside. Make hand prints on a shower curtain with paint mixed with moisturiser, or on a big blackboard with water.

Movers, Shakers and Players

Children (24-36 months)

Children at this stage love doing things with bare feet - try standing in a shallow tray of paint, then walking, running and jumping on a big roll of paper outside (supervise carefully to avoid slipping). Try painting or making letters with fingers only - no brushes. Or trail fingers in paint, then 'walk' them across the paper. Suggest that children hold a fat paintbrush between their toes and try painting with it, or printing/stamping using their feet to hold tools.

Walkers, Talkers and Pretenders

Foundation 1&2 (over 3)

Try offering this! Get a skateboard, children dip hands and feet in paint, lie on the skateboard and propel themselves across paper using hands and feet - and printing a path in hand and feet. Try using more tools with your feet - pencils, crayons, felt pens. Can the children draw or write with their feet? Use a stamp pad to make finger print pictures for cards or letters. Try printing with different parts of hands and feet (elbows, sides of hands, heels, knees) and turning these into pictures by adding lines with a fine felt pen.

Moving on into the Foundation Stage

White boards, clipboards and magnet boards

These simple resources are now popular and familiar in settings and schools. They come in several sizes and types. A5 clipboards and white boards are suitable for work 'on-the-move' while A4 boards give more working room and may be more popular for table top activities. Some boards are combined white and magnet boards. Magnetic strip is useful too.

Young babies may enjoy patting a white-board or removing your marks, but this resource is not really suitable for babies, except for displaying simple pictures or photos, for instance near a cot or resting area.

Heads Up, Lookers and Communicators

Babies (8-18 months)

Simple magnetic shapes on a board, or dry wipe pens for first mark making can be provided for babies to play with and explore. The door from an old fridge, fixed to the wall makes a great magnet board. Display items on magnetic boards by using magnetic strip or button magnets (Google 'magnetic strip' for suppliers). Fridge magnets make good playthings and can be used on a cookie sheet or other metal tray.

Sitters, Standers and Explorers

Young children (18-24 months)

As soon as children can use pens, they will love having clipboards and whiteboards in their play. Offer them indoors and outside for free access, even if they only carry them around! Offer whiteboards also as part of the mark making area equipment, with dry wipe pens, magnetic pictures etc. Use magnets for instant displays that children can do themselves, and for pictorial timetables of daily events. This is particularly helpful for children with special needs.

Movers, Shakers and Players

Children (24-36 months)

Add clipboards and whiteboards to story sacks and creative resource collections, so children can use mark making everywhere. Use the boards in group time to recall events and experiences and to plan trips, visits and future activities, make shopping lists. Record when children have completed activities. Continue the use of magnets and strips for display.

Make a magnet board to display children's mark making and writing at home and in your setting.

Walkers, Talkers and Pretenders

Foundation 1&2 (over 3)

Encourage children to continue the use of whiteboards and clipboards in imaginative play indoors and outside. They may want to take photos or photocopies of their work as a more permanent record. The boards are also very useful for planning and recording the things children intend to do and equipment they may need. Whiteboards and magnet boards are also useful for phonic games, letter, sound and number recognition, alphabet work and letter formation practice, but a wide and creative use is essential.

Moving on into the Foundation Stage

Painting

Painting is a key activity in all early years settings, and one which children really enjoy. Collect a wide range of different equipment and types of paint, and make sure you offer a range of papers and other surfaces to encourage children to develop painting techniques and maintain interest in a familiar activity.

Young babies (0-8 months)

Hold a young baby and let them pat and feel paint in a container. Let them reach out to touch paintings and other pictures. The youngest babies will respond to strong contrasts, particularly black and white designs. They could sit on your knee while you paint wide black stripes down a sheet of white paper, or a simple face, object or other pattern.

Heads Up, Lookers and Communicators

Babies (8-18 months)

Paint on a vertical surface, applied by hand is a great way for babies to experience paint. Or you could sit a baby in the middle of a piece of paper so they can paint around themselves with a big brush. Exploring paint in a builder's tray (with or without a companion) is also a suitably 'hands on' method. Standing babies will enjoy painting on low easels

Sitters, Standers and Explorers

Young children (18-24 months)

At this stage young chidlren may just enjoy the activity of painting, either doing painting after painting, or painting something then covering it with a single colour. They may also destroy paper in their enthusiastic brushing. This is quite a normal way to explore and get used to what paint can do. Offer plenty of paper and simple ways to fix it, so exploration is easy. Add a bit of wallpaper paste to make the paint thicker and encourage the use of fingers and hands!

Movers, Shakers and Players

Children (24-36 months)

Increase the range of papers, paints, brushes and other markers, so children can begin to choose the thickness of brushes and types of paint. Add sticks, feathers, thin cardboard tubes, printing objects, sponges, dabbers etc. Try painting plastic animals, toy cars and other equipment - then wash it off again. Paint on wallpaper rolls, boards on walls and outside, big cardboard boxes from washing machines etc.

Walkers, Talkers and Pretenders

Foundation 1&2 (over 3)

If they have had early experience at independent activities, chidlren will now be able to mix their own paint and select their own brushes and paper from the range you are offering. If you provide water for paint mixing in a liquid soap pump dispenser, it will be much easier for children to control. Try painting with two brushes, or using mixed media - paint, collage, glue, finger paint. Suggest simple pattern making with lines, circles, squares etc, and repeating patterns from left to right on the page, or filling a page with a repeated letter.

Moving on into the Foundation Stage

Mud and sticks

Mud is cheap, fun and ever fascinating for children. Use sterilised compost from a garden centre for the youngest chidlren, and supervise the activity well, so there is no health risk. Older children need to be taught not to put mud in their mouths and to wear suitable clothing for mud work.

Wash hands carefully and supervise the activity well.

Young babies (0-8 months)

Take babies outside to look at older children involved in mud and stick activities. When you are out for walks, notice mud and puddles and talk about them with babies as you carry them or push buggies through them. Hold babies where they can touch mud or compost with fingers and toes. Give them small sticks to hold, wave and drop. Of course all these activities will need close supervision and encouragement from you.

Heads Up, Lookers and Communicators

Babies (8-18 months)

Mud and compost are great resources for messy play with babies. You will need to use sterilised soil or compost and watch carefully because of the habit babies have of exploring everything with their mouths! Once this is done, you can sit one or two babies in a builder's tray with soil or compost, wet or dry. It is usually enough to provide the material itself for squeezing, squashing, patting, poking. Simple spoons and cups can be added as the material becomes more familiar.

Sitters, Standers and Explorers

Young children (18-24 months)

Try to provide a digging area outside where chidlren can just dig - nothing to do with growing things, just digging, shifting, filling and emptying. The area will need a cover to protect it from animals and from getting too wet. Offer child sized trowels, spades, forks, buckets and barrows, and young children will play for ages in this natural, satisfying activity. If you can't provide a permanent digging area, tip a growbag or other bag of soil into a builder's tray or other big container.

Movers, Shakers and Players

Children (24-36 months)

Continue to offer mud play in free choice, but as children get more used to the activity, you could add some more equipment (moulds, buckets, pots, scoops, bun tins etc) and sticks, twigs and small logs to extend the constructions and games they invent. Making mud pies is a traditional game that never fails to fascinate children, so make sure they know about making these. Make the most of walks in wet weather to explore muddy puddles in boots and waterproofs.

Walkers, Talkers and Pretenders

Foundation 1&2 (over 3)

Offer mud play on a large or small scale. Many older children enjoy making gardens and miniature landscapes for small world figures - dinosaurs, animals, people, etc. Building, sculpting and arranging objects all give opportunities for discussion, and for making signs, notices and labels, or for writing stories. Photos of the activities can be made into books or Powerpoint presentations for the computer or whiteboard. Building with sticks, twigs, small logs etc refines hand control, concentration and creativity. Write with sticks and liquid mud on paths, walls or thick card.

Moving on into the Foundation Stage

Tyres and wheels

Big, small, toy or real, wheels make great mark making objects. Make wheel marks on all sorts of surfaces and with all sorts of materials. Children will love them and will come up with new ways of making marks as they get familiar with the methods.

Babies need to become familiar with wheeled vehicles and toys. Make sure they can explore the wheels on toys by watching and touching them. You could also enjoy making marks with pushchairs and prams when you go for a walk.

Heads Up, Lookers and Communicators

Babies (8-18 months)

Little wooden cars with handles or grips on top are good for babies to hold and manipulate. Put a thin layer of sand, flour, paint or gloop in a builder's tray on a low table or the floor, and let them have a go at first track making. If you line the tray with paper, then add a few spoonfuls of paint of different colours, you will get a great picture to display. Try making tracks with toy cars in puddles or small muddy patches outside.

Sitters, Standers and Explorers

Young children (18-24 months)

Put down a big sheet or roll of paper outside. Put a big sponge in an empty ice cream box. Add some paint and use it like a stamp pad for putting paint on wheels of toy cars. Run the cars around on the paper to make tracks and trails. Line a slide with paper and run painty cars down it. Tie strings to small vehicles and let the children run through puddles to make wet tracks, or through mud to make muddy ones. Look at tracks and match with cars.

Movers, Shakers and Players

Children (24-36 months)

At this stage, embark on making tracks with the outdoor wheeled toys. Ride them through puddles and look at the wet tracks, ride them over a carpet tile soaked in paint and over paper or paths. Weave them in and out of the tracks of other toys. Make tracks in mud or sand. Continue to use toy cars and other small vehicles to make tracks and patterns on paper, card, fabric or in gloop, runny clay, paint, rolled out dough etc.

Walkers, Talkers and Pretenders

Foundation 1&2 (over 3)

Children at this stage will enjoy both large and small track making and may get really obsessed with tracks in general. Take photos of tracks of all sorts (birds, shoes and boots, tyres, animals) and display them or make a 'Guess What Made this Track' book. Draw paths and roads on paper to follow with toy cars, using stamp pads or paint to ink the wheels. Explore other ways of making tracks and trails, with drippy bottles, roll-on deodorant bottles filled with paint, marbles or small balls rolled in a paddling pool, marble runs and tubes.

Moving on into the Foundation Stage

Spray, drip and drizzle

Small hand held sprays are a cheap and effective way to make some different marks. Get them from garden centres and DIY stores - look for ones with easy grips and triggers, suitable for small hands and fingers. Or get some cheap spray tops for plastic water or pop bottles from www.twowests.co.uk and make your own sprays.

Young babies (0-8 months)

Show babies how sprays work by demonstrating them yourself. Spray on mirrors, windows and even gently on their hands, feet or legs. Some babies love this, others may not be so sure!

Take babies out to see older children spraying and spray painting in the garden.

Heads Up, Lookers and Communicators

Babies (8-18 months)

The gripping trigger action may be too hard for small hands, so you could offer some simple spraying bath toys. Ducks and other toys that squirt and spray will help with grasp and squeezing, strengthening the hand and finger muscles needed for holding mark making tools. Squeezing and spraying bath toys can be offered in paddling pools and water trays. Try Googling 'bath toys' for suppliers or ask parents and friends for cast-offs.

Sitters, Standers and Explorers

Young children (18-24 months)

Get some tops for water bottles, as these are easier and softer to squeeze than garden sprayers. Let children experiment and investigate these simple sprayers in water trays or freely outside. This sort of action gives good muscle building practice in gripping and holding. Try drawing simple targets or circles with chalk on paths and walls for aiming practice, and use the sprays to water plants or for adding water to mix gloop and dough.

Movers, Shakers and Players

Children (24-36 months)

Introduce small, hand-held sprays when children can cope with them, continuing to offer bottles and spray toys too. Hang up big sheets of paper or a shower curtain, and add some food colouring to the water in the sprays for a spraying activity out of doors; or paint a wall with white paint for spraying, then wash it down with a hose. Using sprays to add water to paint, dough, clay and other malleable materials will give practice to hand muscles and control to the water supply.

Walkers, Talkers and Pretenders

Foundation 1&2 (over 3)

Continue to offer sprays with water and paint play as child initiated activities. Add different sorts of smaller plastic sprays such as perfume and cosmetics sprays (look in chemists' shops and supermarkets). Children will enjoy having a range of different paint colours in sprays, so they can create their own spray pictures. Paint or food colouring also make great pictures and patterns on small pieces of fabric. Use sprays of paint to colour clay or dough models after baking, or spray over loose objects on paper to make spray outlines or silhouettes.

Moving on into the Foundation Stage

Labels and names

Making and using labels is a good way to start mark making for a purpose. Buy luggage labels from stationers, or make your own. Use computer labels and stickers (both plain and printed) to encourage children to name and label objects and belongings.

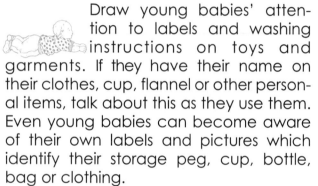

Draw young babies' attention to labels and washing instructions on toys and garments. If they have their name on their clothes, cup, flannel or other personal items, talk about this as they use them. Even young babies can become aware of their own labels and pictures which identify their storage peg, cup, bottle, bag or clothing.

Continue to draw babies' attention to the way objects and places are labelled - labels above their pegs, names on their lunch boxes or cups, names on their pictures and other creations. Look at labels on equipment drawers and other storage. Make badges and stickers for them with pictures and their name on.

Young children (18-24 months)

Keep using labels (with pictures and words) for equipment, places, objects and belongings. If the chidlren have their own peg, locker or drawer for personal things, let them help to make the labels by decorating or adding pictures or borders to their names with felt pens or crayons. Encourage them to choose their own activities with your help from clearly labelled drawers and boxes with picture clues or even a piece of the equipment stuck on with a glue gun.

Movers, Shakers and Players

Children (24-36 months)

Labels are also a key way of helping children with clearing up and putting things away, so make sure the children are involved in making and understanding labels. Use tie-on parcel labels to identify objects and props for stories. Label drinking cups or bottles, outdoor clothing and boots, equipment and activities - collections of water and sand toys, pots of pens, crayons, pencils, and praise children when they return items to the correct container.

Walkers, Talkers and Pretenders

Foundation 1&2 (over 3)

At this stage, encourage children to label and name their own models, pictures and other work. Offer folded card for stand up labels so children can write their own names and details independently or with your help. Children can label their own pegs and drawers themselves, using letters, patterns and pictures. Make labels and notices to help with organisation, such as '3 people in the sand' or 'hang your clipboard here'. Try self registration with name cards, or you could use labels to inspire talking and storying by putting a label round a soft toy or puppet.

Moving on into the Foundation Stage

35

Messages, letters and cards

From the earliest age, babies and children can and should have access to materials for making and sending messages, cards and letters. Provide a rich and stimulating mark making area in your setting and join the children as they work and play with the materials you offer. This doesn't have to be expensive!

Sit with babies, letting them watch you as you make cards, write notes, or make lists and reminders. Talk about what you are doing, naming the equipment and describing what you do. The activity does not have to be making a card for the baby - modelling mark making, cutting, writing and using simple tools is an important part of preparing babies for the activities they will be involved in later.

Heads Up, Lookers and Communicators

Once they are on the move, babies will enjoy getting involved in tearing, sticking, making marks and screwing paper. Provide plenty of easy to use materials - tissue paper, big crayons, glue sticks (when they are ready). Sit with them and help them to manage the materials - don't direct them, just let them explore. When you make cards for special occasions, let babies make their own marks and stick on stickers of torn paper.

Sitters, Standers and Explorers

Young children (18-24 months)

Continue to extend the range of materials for making messages and cards. Add pictures from magazines, wrapping paper and stickers. Offer glue sticks, washable felt pens and other markers. Let children have free access to the materials and respond enthusiastically to their creations. As children get used to making their own cards and greetings, they will be able and willing to make cards for friends and family members as well as for special occasions and celebrations.

Movers, Shakers and Players

Children (24-36 months)

At this stage, add envelopes (used ones are fine), sticky and tie-on labels, and coloured and shaped papers and cards. As children begin to use scissors, include these, but don't expect complex cutting activities - simply snipping strips of paper is absorbing to many chidlren at this stage. Letters are fascinating things - some children will fold and deliver pieces of paper and card without marking or drawing, just delivering!

Walkers, Talkers and Pretenders

Foundation 1&2 (over 3)

At this stage, children will enjoy exploring all sorts and types of equipment and resources for writing and mark making - messages, cards, notes and invitations - envelopes, hole punches, staplers, shaped scissors, labels, wrapping paper, lists of names, string, tape etc. Let them help to make a simple posting box or individual pigeon holes so children can begin to send messages to each other and to you. This will give them reasons for writing and practising the skills you are teaching them. Adding a computer may attract reluctant writers.

Moving on into the Foundation Stage

Places, people and stories

Making up stories is a vital start to storying, Begin with naming people and places, and recalling events. Babies and children need to practise their own real-life stories verbally and in pictures before they begin to draw and write them for real. A digital camera and a good supply of high quality story books are essential ingredients to successful storying.

Young babies (0-8 months)

Babies need to think through the things that happen to them, and they need your help until they have the vocabulary and language to do it themselves. Don't forget that just because babies can't talk, they can't think and remember! Talk about everything you do together. Plan, anticipate and return to events and activities. Make quiet times where you can just talk or look at books with one or two babies in a relaxed atmosphere.

Heads Up, Lookers and Communicators

Babies (8-18 months)

Continue to talk about events and activities before, during and after they happen. Take lots of photos so you can name and describe activities, visits, friends and family members. Make photo books (plastic photo books are more robust for dribblers and chewers), and collect familiar photos on the computer so babies can look at them frequently with your help. Looking at lots of picture books, and talking about events and activities, will also pre-pare babies for making their own stories.

Sitters, Standers and Explorers

Young children (18-24 months)

Continue to make photo records of key people, places, events and activities, and use these in conversations, for making books and for telling the everyday stories of life in your setting. Give young children plenty of opportunities to tell their own stories. Some of these will be told as they play, some will be about drawings, paintings, models they make. Writing down what they say gives status and value to their story telling, so offer this service to them for labelling pictures, writing captions and stories.

Movers, Shakers and Players

Children (24-36 months)

Offer plenty of paper, mark making equipment and other stimuli, such as little booklets of paper, zigzag books, stapled pads etc. Help them to make books from photos, catalogue pictures, drawings. Continue to act as a scribe for them, but encourage them to make their own mark making attempts. Display their books in the book corner so other children can read them. Make photo collections of people and places, and of visits, walks and visitors.

Walkers, Talkers and Pretenders

Foundation 1&2 (over 3)

Story telling and story making really take off at this stage. With plenty of early experience, children will make books and illustrate them with enthusiasm. You just need to provide plenty of materials and stimulating experiences, and be an appreciative audience! Story telling sessions are an important element - give children time to tell their own 'real-life' or imaginary stories to friends and to adults. Let them take digital photos of friends and activities to make photo books with simple captions. Use Powerpoint to make story presentations for computers and whiteboards.

Moving on into the Foundation Stage

Existing and planned titles in the Baby and Beyond series include:

* **Messy Play** (ready now)
* **Sensory Experiences** (ready now)
* **Music and Sound** (ready now)
* **The Natural World** (ready now)
* **Construction** (ready now)
* **Marks & Mark Making** (ready now)
* **Puppets, Soft Toys & Dolls** (2007)

* **Bikes, Prams & Pushchairs** (2007)
* **Cooking** (2007)
* **Finger Songs and Rhymes** (2007)
* **Small World Play** (2007)
* **Stories, Songs, Rhymes** (2007)
* **Riding Together** (2008)
* **Role Play** (2008)